Copyright © 2020 by **Rebel Fleur**

All rights reserved. No part of this publication may be reproduced, distributed or transmitted in any form or by any means, without prior written permission.

Rebel Fleur/Self Published
PO BOX 421
East Meadow, New York 11554

Publisher's Note: This is a work of fiction. Names, characters, places, and incidents are a product of the author's imagination. Locales and public names are sometimes used for atmospheric purposes. Any resemblance to actual people, living or dead, or to businesses, companies, events, institutions, or locales is completely coincidental.

Library of Congress United States of America 2020

Loss Love & Life/ Rebel Fleur. -- 1st ed.
ISBN 978-0578690056

I0087063

Preface

Life has a way of making decisions for you. I had been going through a difficult time and then COVID-19 hit and suddenly what had already been a tough season started to feel unbearable and coping was challenging. My body took ill from intolerable stress and fighting began to feel futile. So, I did what I always do. I started to write in a personal blog, writing every day, multiple times a day to process my emotions uncensored. When I shared a piece or two with a couple of friends I was asked "when is the second book coming?" That's when I realized the blog was the second book. And it was time to birth it as a new collection. It is never easy sharing my work because it comes from such a personal place. But my hope is that others' will connect to the truth of themselves within it. One thing is clear to me. We are all human and feel all things but occasionally we need permission to accept those feelings. I want you to know you are not alone, and I hope by reading this you feel connected and that you have permission to *feel* it *all*.

Prologue

Paradox of a Thug Dove

She is a gentle soul wrapped in fire fierce.
Her gaze can pierce the truth, buried deep
Third eye sees and she frees
others to peace in her atmosphere.
She cares not in perfection
But in the reflection of growth.
Dope mystery encased
In a sexy sensual space
Her mind quantifies that God is Real.
See her deal isn't
you get over but rather
Grace stands boulder
And if you don't know...
Then you'll never know.... her...
A good thing.
xo

Thank you, God, for the gift of artistic expression.
It is oxygen to my soul.

Dedicated to the arts in this unprecedented time.
To the unicorns often misunderstood with hearts vast as the
sea. Lovers of transparency exhausted by bullshit.
Humanity and its many colors.

*And the **Wolf**, my twin flame,*
popcorn, Netflix and sweatpants, love Bonita.

*I have only ever completely been **in love** with two.*
Both dubious timing.
Both I would have extracted the stars from the heavens for.

***The first**-beautiful standard set-children always believe it's*
forever. '99

***The second-**beautiful mix of what moves my soul and unlocks a*
restricted heart. '19

Timing can be a mysterious, mercurial game of life.

4

Musings

LIFE

LOVE

LOSS

RENEWEL/REVELATIONS

Rebel Fleur

There is much to discover about life and self in the stillness and silence.
When a seed is planted it grows under the soil.
Covered in a dark space where light and water must find room to penetrate for growth.
*In **time** something beautiful emerges from the darkness.*

Loss Love & Life

Loss love and life…
I look to the sky to find the dotted lines
connecting the reflections
Of what I knew
what I know
and it's all a mystery.
I hurt in places deep often never seen.
And the mix of flows, hold on and let go
To grow
Feels like a blow to everything I've known.
It's the capture of my heart in a cage... hidden away
Cause the rage and pain of release
cuts
Like knives through fresh flesh
These tests
Deplete my soul
blood turns cold.
And I want to unfold in a space between heaven and earth
Where nothing hurts.
Because it's becoming too much.
Rivers run in reverse, even the earth hurts
And I'm stuck asking why
I see trees cry and politicians lie while people die.
So, I get high to forget, close my eyes to regrets
And debts.
Listen to a beat that reminds me
Hearts beat…

But losing you and losing you then losing you and losing them
then get back up and get back up and get back up again

PLEASE
PAUSE

Can I close my eyes and fly?
Do a reprise of this confusion
Do a transfusion of love into the pulse
Flip the direction create a new infection
That transfers darkness to light and beauty back to community

Yeah immunity to the bullshit.
And I admit
I - am - all- over- the - place
Looking for grace to hold my sanity
While I'm missing … and missing and still missing
Wishing I understood what I can't
And this plan feels unjust.
I mean I can't even touch….
Yet I'm still grabbing for peace like oxygen
Fighting for my life, wanting to win.
Even when I can only depend on what I can't
See
The God in me.
Still hurting, still searching.
Battered bruised and confused
Trusting that something new will bloom
And beauty will begin, again.
Loss love and life…

If I never get to say it again.

I love you.

The Truth Nobody Sees - Tired

Created to do service
That is my purpose
But I get tired
not always wired
To keep going without
Falling
No place to really lean
Days without being seen
Building blocks with what I got
Hoping the clock doesn't stop
And time doesn't run out
My doubts try to get loud
Because it's only me.

And running free isn't an option
And I never really mention
The everyday tension
In my body and mind.
And sometimes I wanna hide
Die a little more on the inside
Holding onto faith and my everyday grace
That keeps me floating
But quietly I'm hoping
For a moment
Someone stronger than I
For me to lay beside
Reassure my broken pieces
That it all has meaning
and to keep on
That my song is not out of tune
And that there is still room for
This weight to be removed
From my plate.
All the sacrifices seen and unknown
I can feel certain regrets have grown
And reconciling them
Appear empty like a home never known...
Every level of the have and have nots
Hard at work

And I'm wondering if this wheel may
Ever stop.
I'm strong.... I'm resilient
because I must be...
but I have a deeper need
as my insides bleed

I'm tired.

Choose Light

Sometimes you have to stitch the sunshine back into cobalt veins and let the rays melt steely wings of the butterfly, unnatural.
You have to fight the urge to destroy false prophets decorated in ornaments of benevolence but undercover the worst kind of assailant.
You have to close your eyes to the truth or risk letting the storm inside your broken soul take down resolve and unbridle it on the arrogance doused in placating, greeting you.
You have to choose the light when it would be too easy to choose the dark.

Red Blue and Black

Red white and black bleeds
Blue dreams under the hands that
Demean those that look like me.
Never said it would be easy
But you're too breezy in taking our lives
Everybody has rights
Except African descent
the cement that built your country
From the bottom up
But we the ones still stuck trying to
Gain a buck from lying with thieves
And lying for thieves
Our soul heaves clouds with black
Smoke that seek to choke out pain
That gained access to our brains
Manipulation is a game that takes time
An insidious rhyme that you started
But we charted through repetition
The mission
Those thoughts are not really ours
tracks on scars never healed.
This deal leaves us still as slaves
Graves filled with dreams deferred
Cause you only meant us to serve
You.

Sapphire Earth

Sapphire unlocks the secrets of what's hidden in a person's
soul.
Unintended-simply
She mends,
a healer that kisses ones' judge within
with
Forgiving touches that grants permission,
To live.
Her eyes look at the subject and anyone could see
She believes
Angels and stars break bread with thee
a piece of her heart
sat in thy hand
oblivious
A thousand rivers flow
And a memory it becomes
Once friend now stranger who knows her stories,
Both mind and on skin
Fire of fragility
sensuality.
Exposed.
Uniquely.
An aqua blue crowns her ocean,
requests of herself that she hadn't...
but time looks not back
instead recognition to process
submission to sunlight and toes submerged on white pearl
shores
earth speaks in its subtle way yet grand beauty.
Seagulls execute a ballet above her head to the hum of crashing
waves serenades.
It is the movie in her sky
While some broken fragments of days untold wash up by her
feet...
And she wonders...
The affectionate warmth of the sun will soon descend, and her
bliss of the moment will pass.
But moon will open its sleeping eyes and capture her in its
enthralling, tempting glow

That beckons to bring its own magic.
Life and its fascinating glory....
Is both the comings and goings, the tears and the smiles, the lasting and forgotten.
The moment that is, the moment that was.
With loose fingers...Sapphire plunges hers delicately in the sand
And watches it slowly trickle down through...
She smiles from its shimmer, it's sensation, the warmth in her hand...
And with the last bit in her palm, she lets a tear fall
it's mixture, brilliant, crystal like pieces of sand encased in a glistening tear.
She remembers thee with reverie
her hand tilts and slowly she watches her makeshift gem cascade into the abyss of particles and vanish.
And she leaves with her footprints in the sand.

Sullen Lullaby Drained

Silent whispers
Prayers quietly conveyed
Red ribbons of sorrow
Sanctions the heart
Beat
Donny Hathaway
Bellows in the wind
In the alone
ears hear what
Pumping valves want to hide
But there is no space or time
That can deny
Roaming waters
Dancing beads
on beauty downcast
In pain and drain
Sullen lullaby from within
Caresses her to sleep.

Today I felt fear creep into my spirit like a thief. Taking up residence like a loud colleague you bumped into who just won't shut up or go away.

Detached. That's how I do life. But I'm not. Yet I am. And I'm seeing it more as I mourn for people I love or even people I don't know dealing with loss. I've had my own and know too well the sorrow it brings. But for me it's something deeper, greater, hard to articulate and understand. If I did drugs or drank on a regular basis, I would escape my pain with them. Perhaps that's why I don't because I know I would. Addictive personality and a creature of habit but not, I follow structure but slightly impulsive. Yep a walking talking fucking contradiction.

I'll never forget it. I was about 16 years old; I think that is about right and I had a best friend down the block from me. She was like my sister and our dads were buddies. They chopped it up big time. Sitting in their lime green and white folding chairs in front of the garage on a scorching hot summer day, drinking their Budweiser beers and leaving a sip in the can for me and my friend. It's no wonder she and I didn't become bloated alcoholics as kids. Our dads had great fun together and her dad was always like my second dad. Talk about a sense of humor. He was bold, and bossy, loving and filled with truth. His wisdom never sounded like a fortune cookie but rather just don't do no dumb shit. To this day I still don't know what really happened. But he started losing weight and he was becoming moody and mean. I remember my girl really upset about it and having to get away from him because it was too much sometimes. Then one night she was sent by her mom to stay the night with me and I just remember the grown-ups talking. She and I played sega (YEAH THAT WAS OUR 16...damn times change) and took polaroid pictures pretending to be famous people. We went to bed thinking all was well with the world. The next morning in the eerie quiet of daybreak my dad woke us up to tell us the news. My besties dad was gone. I remember her shock and silence and I began to wail. Something in me collapsed. I have a haze on what happened next other than lots of running around and my friend with us so her mom and family could take care of things. She finally went

16

home a couple days later, and I was to see her again at the service. I walked into the church and from the distance I could see him lying there, still, silent, not laughing, not hugging me, not telling dirty jokes, not like I knew, and I ran out. I couldn't do it.

This was the beginning of a massive shift into detachment. I no longer wanted to feel that kind of pain ever again, so I grew distant to things and people I loved. They are all going to leave me anyway at some point so why bother. Every loss since then I have found myself more numb. I won't allow anyone next to me close enough to hurt when they will eventually vanish from my life. I don't know how to reconcile this part of life and it scares me greatly. I'm realizing it's also part of the reason I choose to be single. I love my parents with everything in me, but I keep emotional distance a lot. I can close myself up. My heart loves hard and deeply and stripping away those people feels like a pain I can't handle. I lean on no one; I can be quite cold if I think it will protect me from the pain of loss.

Today I cried like a child...the level of pain that has just been sitting buried in me wanting to come pouring out. And yes, I let it happen and then I felt myself zip back up again. Why? because the emotions are so heavy and painful that they feel suffocating and overwhelming. How can it not be when you love and care so intensely? I swear sometimes I wish I didn't. This life would not only be easier, but I would blend in a lot better... with the fuck them and I didn't care anyway and oh well and that's life and next mantras. Cancel culture bullshit. Straight up fucking alien walking on earth is what I am. My heart hurts because of the loss. My heart hurts because of what I may never have. My heart hurts because of the love I desire and require, rare and yet my heart says staying away is good because you'll never know the pain of losing any of it. I let someone deep in my heart recently then I guess I lost him though I didn't ever really have him, and that pain was daunting. And the pain didn't really go away but I just got cold in a different way. Do I love in general...when you have a heart like mine it's hard not to love so yes, I do but from a far distance. And no one gets in. Detached, at least enough to keep going.

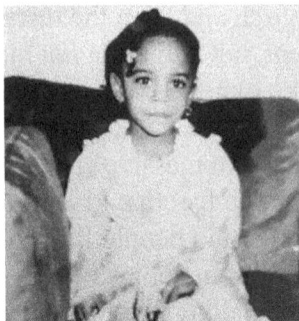

When I look at her there is a space in my womb that longs and cries. She reminds me of the mother I dream of being and the little girl whose eyes would look up at me and call me mommy. I always pictured this angel like beauty whose curiosity and innocence would melt my heart. This blessing that I could pour my love and soul into. She reminds me of the brokenness that lived in that little version of myself. The shame of being different and the never-ending battle of never feeling like enough. How often she was picked on and left to her own imagination because kids didn't want to play with the little girl with the crooked legs. She reminds me of the beginning stages of taking pen to paper and trying to articulate pain through words... The lonely rose, that was a first and a good one, but my teacher's note said beautiful work but to stay away from clichés not realizing I was crying out for help. This little girl reminds me of hopes and dreams and love in its purist form. And today I wish I could go back and love her a little harder a little stronger and tell her that she doesn't ever have to stop being her. But since I can't I look at my reflection in the mirror and see her staring back at me helpless and confused and I say "It's ok. I got you and I love you."

Love letter to her:

Dear Little Me,
Inquisitive, observant, loving and unique. If I could go back in time and hold your hand, hug you tight and tell you how much I love you I would but I can't so I am writing you this letter because there are so many things you didn't know and I wish you was told back then. With abundant love and tears in my eyes I am looking back at your partially cripple, collapsing

18

knees and little frame at 6 years old, with tenderness, arms wide to embrace you and share with you the secrets you should know. In life you will have struggles and trials…but meet them with grace and not bitterness, even when you cry, know that your journey will be a testimony and healing for others. Your difficulties will impregnate upon you an empathetic heart. You will fight and support the disadvantage, the underdogs and those who yet know how to express themselves. You will see others potential and help them grow into their greater selves. It will be an honor for your eyes to witness. Your tests will prepare you on how to talk to the hurting and relate on a personal level that they can respond to. When you look in the mirror though you may wish to lay out in the sun to become like the golden and darker hued girls you so admire, love what you see. Even the crippled knees. I know it will be tough through the taunts and teases, but trust God has a plan for you and what you see will grow and blossom. Your design is authentic and original to you. Fall in love with her. Because without it you may fall into traps and deceit that can leave damage hard to recover from. Don't yearn to be anyone else or live their life, because what God has as theirs belongs to only them and vice versa. Let your beauty also come from within. Be kind, considerate and loving to all people. Every person has purpose and requires love. Learn to fight for yourself and use your verbal skills to not only diffuse heightened situations but as a tool to cope with what you experience. Look at your parents and family with the eyes of humanity for they are frail and broken and not pillars of perfection. Each one comes from their own separate circumstances and are works in progress, loving the best way that they know how. Offer support and show gratitude with compassion to understand and not take sides but be a voice of reason. Regarding friendships, understand what that word really means. People come and go in your life offering blessings and lessons that sometimes will offend and sometimes will make you smile but they are only there for a specific purpose and go. Friendships are vastly different. They are seeds planted deep with roots that continue to mature over time. You have different seasons of engaging, but they are a foundational structure that doesn't whither in the storms of life. A friend will support your truth from a place of love. Dependable and consistent, they will listen with their heart. Understand that they too have limitations and respect that, however if their limitations bruise, dis-honor or disrespect who you are. It is your duty to stand firm and state your case with grace. If embraced, be gracious to know such a person if not, it is time to part ways and not judge but know this doesn't serve you in a healthy way. Never be ashamed or made to feel shamed for doing such. Recognize that consistency or lack of is reflective of character, do not ignore it nor judge it but position yourself accordingly. Watch what people do as oppose to what they say. Words that sound good with no action are empty and will only cause you disappointment. You will love and love deeply but be selective and know that anyone worth being with will earn your love. Do not give yourself freely. If someone is not willing to support your trials or be there when you need then they do not warrant your joys and gifts of love. Be careful not to pour too much of yourself into another person so not to become depleted and forget your own desires and dreams. You deserve to be cared for and poured into as well. Your wounds will make you resistant to trust anyone too quickly, this is a gift. It protects you from nonsense. In choosing a mate, choose one who will see the strength in all your scars and challenges, see the beauty in your vulnerability when your guard is down, respect your toughness and understand, see the lover and know that she is reserved for him only. If you are to be hurt by love…as much as you want to throw in the towel, don't. You may make what you think are mistakes, you may not see everything all the time but trust your heart knows what it knows. Bring light into those you love lives' and love because you choose not out of obligation. If it isn't returned from where you show love always know that God can bless you from other places and persons. Do not turn bitter on love deferred nor blame yourself as unworthy because of outcomes. Give 110% of what you believe in and continue forward with no regrets. Never stop being who you are but know when to let go. In your career fight with vigilance to do what you love. Believe in your abilities and work hard. Keep ethics and quality first. Use the experiences you will have and the tools that God has given you and make them work. Your calling is not just about being an artist, but you are an advocate for many different causes. The right roles will be tailored just for you because it will accentuate your greater purpose. It will not be easy, but your dream is possible and let no one tell you otherwise, not even yourself. As you go through tests of health, life and family, you will begin to grow weary and doubtful…STAND UP and recognize you are just being sharpened for an unbelievable testimony. You will walk it alone and many you wanted to be by you side, wont. But it's ok my sweet because God has never and will never leave you. Cry your tears and feel your pain but continue to pursue through it. Never give up on you! Fight for what you know is right. No matter where you are placed, keep your integrity and give the best of you. When the need to half ass comes upon you it is time to go. That is not your truth. Go hard or go home. Remember you are beautiful and unique just as you are. You don't have to change or fit into anyone's mold to achieve. You come from a hot-tempered background…keep your cool. Speak with assertiveness and respect but when you feel the flood of anger come over you from others behavior…PAUSE, breathe and work it out when you are in the right frame of mind. Don't hold on to people who don't want to be held on to. And don't bottle up your feelings. It is better to resolve with class and walk away then to knock the crap out of someone…:)

Be bold and dynamic and fear nothing. Always know that in you beats the heart of a warrior. Nothing is in vain. Don't run from who you are but cultivate every distinct part of yourself…including the controversial and primal. You will blend your many colors well. They ALL serve your light. The odds will seem stacked against you from the very start, but you will prove to be a resilient spitfire that will continue on.

xoxoxo
Your Future
(meet me in the batcave…that's where I'm hanging these days)

Rebel Fleur

Paradox

It is the paradox that beckons questions
one soul
Polar opposites living within, simultaneously
both true
There is no lie in the many...
though in this examination only two addressed
she sun, above the earth
moon beneath the waters...
the heights are high. the depths are deep.
Feed the need
Both sides.
Ordinary suffocates her breathing
Need the language of imaginations, passion filled hues
a mind of equal destination and poignant thoughts
that teaches and brims with adventure...
A slow infusion learns.
It is also lighthearted ease
a sweet kiss laminates the blood pumping valve/
as where the trigger of love flickers
Pandora's box unlocked.
decadence released...
primal, pretty beast, light splintering the dark
contradiction but not.
It is the crawl on silk, backdrop in low amber
No rules or regulations... holder of flame
It is that spark... that awakens primitive, submissive
Angel and Vixen, vying for permission to FULLY respire.
Danger in pleasure filled fingertips and lips...
a heart pure that drips good intentions/
Senses, titillating high
loyal to appetite and affection / urges
in direct opposition, but true.
There is no lie
equal
Iridescent eyes won't run from herself
piercing fire courtesan
adoring loyal partner
the various shades in between
it is a melting pot of much...

22

languid yet contained...
the paradox questions...
define?
The rainbow of her soul.

Rebel Fleur

The Division

blood stained suits
white cellophane gloves
best laid plans for the
black man, king
the women can't see
queen she can never be
dissension
there is no intervention
brown paper bag test inside the family
fail
self-hate
escalates
when the mind is gone
to the cleverness
insidious system
designed to destroy
seeds planted with crumbs from a table of no joy
eat it up, false validation
dollar and cents cashing out on souls
recovery of the spirit all time low
look mommy there is a golden bullet with my name
no shame when the dictator claims that's all there's to gain
and like toy soldiers we fall
in the streets, in the home, in the food chain of life
who the fuck said we had to get permission to have what's
right?
It's time to stop playing checkers in a game of chess
And take authority of our divine best…
That doesn't ask but recognizes
we don't have to be accepted IN TO
To be respected TO DO…
Take the power back that has always been…
ours to release
When we break the chains to please…
Be free to the beauty
a culture rich in traditions
Refusing to be marginalized by opinion
of anyone BUT SELF.

Reprogram, flip the game on itself and put the projected versions of us
On the shelf.
Machine watching and laughing cause it ain't gotta work too hard,
Masters of confusion
Create intrusions of delusions
They tell us what's in season
Then we start judging each other
And don't understand the reason….
LOOK…
Waging war…the battle is within
Manifested external destruction
So, we're boxing with no one else in the ring
shadow
It's like treating a symptom but ignoring what's at the marrow.
it's time to stop drinking what we've been told
And start actualizing what we know…
Powerful beyond measure when we own it.
The system knows it.
And when we show it.
They must bow down
before it.
Our greatness recognized by us FIRST.
Then game over.
CHECKMATE!

Rebel Fleur

Take A Chance On You

As human beings it's easy to settle. Unfulfilled jobs, relationships, life. Fear of the unknown can debilitate. Money can blind. I found out what I was really made of when I took on a project and things about the circumstances didn't feel right in my soul. I was incredibly unhappy, but the money was good, and people tried to make it right, yet I felt like I was settling against my own heart. So, I stood my ground (by God's grace) and graciously walked away. And although I didn't know what would come next, the freedom, release of the burden of unhappiness and being unfulfilled lifted from me. Could I have stayed...that would have been an infraction against myself and then my inevitable unhappiness would have been because I didn't have the courage to stand for me. We never really know what's in store for ourselves unless we become courageous and willing to believe that there is better, soul inspiring better, joy, happiness and release, stop settling for what doesn't support that because it's safe. Be brave, be bold. Don't look back with regrets. Don't wake up after time, stuck because you didn't give yourself a chance. I'm not saying it's easy but settling can deceive with "ohh there is so much to lose" and yet oh there is so much to gain. Peace of mind, freedom and happiness is priceless.

Naked Human

How beautiful the bitter taste of time
It's amazing how much we can conjure up to mask
The reflection of hurt…
Tough, heavy handed external shields branded bitter
Harsh lips of vulgar spewing's the cynics lullaby
Ambivalent dives of it's all good. Nonchalant submerging
Into the attention of that which we don't seek.
Blame and question character of what you knew was true
Only to hide from...
Fear
Of I miss you, or I cried, or I'm sorry, or I'm confused
Only to not look stupid, or desperate or needy or weak.
But in times we are all these, and how magnificent
I run from vulnerability so not to be exposed
I run from what makes us human.
I have run myself in circles…and I laugh and cry
with and at myself simultaneously.
There's a point on this kaleidoscope of life
That I must stop and breathe in the real
For it is beautifully bare and open, raw and blemished
It is a piece of honesty, untouched, unapologetic and all
human.
It is this piece of humanity often determined as ugly and
unacceptable.
But I reprise to accept what lingers in the fear
Because it is in God's divine order to have balance
I am not always smart, I make faulty choices
I am not always confidant, I may crave assurance
I am not always right; I have to ask for forgiveness
I am not always strong and may need a shoulder.
I am not perfect but always beautiful.
It is this simplistic truth that breeds compassion and
understanding.
I admit boldly that I have tried to save face to shield my pain
For fear of looking human.
I admit I have beat myself up emotionally for being human
But in truth there is no gain or protection in either.
Only a deception of the mind that seeks to gratify the ego
momentarily.

But gathered in the solar plexus reality ruminates.
How can I be honest if I hide the emotional truth?
Come tears you're real
I would lose the moment of growth
Avoidance breeds a bubbling battlefield below the surface
My reality no longer brims but breathes on the surface.
I. Am. Naked. Human.

*There is a difference between loving and being **in love***
The latter seeks to build a future.
Love for a thug dove is a spiritual provocation of the soul.
It does not seek but surrenders to the existence of an
undeniable connection.
Never duplicated and not often found
Unicorns respond to magic.
(spiritual, intellectual, playful, emotional and sexual)
Unapologetically so.

29

It is the unexpected that has a way of tripping up the beat.
No intention to mix melodies but rather flow to her own
rhythm
But sometimes like solar particles something unseen by the eye
Collides and the contradiction arises, she can't
but magnetized she will.
These particles that pull at that unknown yet known.
She bleeds in a part he can't see, or can he?
She is no sport and yet the games of the day deceive.
Players conceive ways to get next.
But blocked before the shot. They average none on her court.
Who is he?
Internal pleads don't.
Look up before you drown, look in before you give voice to a
choice
That you can't erase.
Too late... his eyes see constellations
hers
See femininity exposed to his deep browns from her hazel
pools
Melting in hands that feel like they have traveled her before.
Take a breath… Each inhale inviting space for him without real
invitation.
Yet setting limitations feels futile.
It's beautiful to exchange dances with lips that know her secret
language
Laughter at ease with just being.
she can't see or can she.
Illusions? Delusions?
That in the forbidden something honest can take place?
She doesn't know him, yet the deeper connect begs her
To protect.
passion neglects to hear the call and she's struck by the beauty
in the flaw.
High from his taste, looking at his face…the longing to grace
him in bliss
Starting with a kiss. What is it about this...?
Man leaving cracks in her shield.
Saturating her body and soul...

as if it was just as it should be.
Touching chakras with fullness of him deep.
She can't complete this equation in any fashion that doesn't
negate.
Pieces of her
Floating in a blur
cornered
by her own shadow
Decadent and delicious, reasoning stands aside
Mind body and heart on an unsettling ride
And wondering why…
Can she…
Will she
Get off
Even the thought
Wants to rage war.
She wants to explore... more of him
Her sin yet so sweet
And this is the cost of this
Unexpected melody
mixing with her beat.

Rebel Fleur

Magic

You were a piece of magic
It is the magical, undefined
That brings about rainbows
And unicorns and rabbits out of
Magician's hats
It is cotton candy covered clouds
On frosty days.
Pretty is a dime a dozen
But magical is unforgettable
It surpasses external musings
And possesses impact that lingers
Like first kisses
Sunsets on pink sand horizons.
Snow angels on freshly fallen frozen flakes.
It takes your breath away without you knowing
Until you catch a glimmer of the mundane
And you recognize that you've been
Struck with a magical, specific to one's own unique cravings.
I save a quiet space for you.
Deleting stardust planted in my spirit
Feels almost impossible. But...
Tears run like rapids because it knows
What my heart doesn't want to see.
Magical is rare...and it is the only fuel of my soul, it's mirror.
It responds to nothing less.
Yet I was mesmerized where my eyes
had no permission to see, but it called to me.
And all that sparkle and flare that lit
A blaze instinctively... I can't repeat.
So tonight, I close my eyes filled with oceans
And dream of magical gleaming with gratitude
while particles of my heart splinters and showers
a brilliant cacophony of
Beauty and heartache.

Explicit I Wanna

No apologies for my beast unleashed
Walking wet through these streets
Cause you still pulsing through me
I'm fantasizing when we're gonna meet
So, you can undue this heat
I wanna fuck and fight and maybe cry
All in the same night.
Perhaps crass but I want my lush ass in your hands
Hip to hip make me drip
Taste my waist
69 on my mind cause my sweet lips
Want to dine
on all of you
Sex walls still throb cause
She remembers, feels you hard
deep thrust
Combination of love and lust
My trust
Wants you to bust inside me
Yeah, I'm feeling nasty and free
Cause these words are my only release
Ride you slow and steady
I want devour in the shower...
hours of pent up appetite...
laying up at night... fingers between my thighs
visualizing you in my mind....
cum so blissfully deliriously I feed
my need through memories...
like a fiend it's intoxicating
there is no debating I am hating not having you near
my thumb imagines yours with four fingers
explore
Masturbating on you, tie me to the bed
while giving me head... make me scream out your name
tame me and inflame me to behave
I want you to take me your way.

And today... this is all I have to say.

33

What Would It?

What would it look like?
If I could love you complete
Take the dream to reality
Do the impossible
Make love in public with our eyes
No lies
Hear them when they say I want you
Deep inside.
Sunsets with breakfast
Reverse the frequencies and be
Free
Healing after a long day
Just lay in my earth and be birthed
Again... Stronger brighter.
Knowing you got a rider
fighter to do the battle by your side.
What would it look like?
If I could love you complete
Take ecstasy of the mind to another level
As we revel in philosophy's and
Uncovering God's decree
How dope would that be.
Transformation of our entire being
Exhale inhale with me slowly
As we touch silently without hands.
What would it look like?
If I could love you complete
Share the bare of our souls
Embraced in the face of one another
No fear.
But released in sobriety with peace.
What would it look like?
If I could love you complete
Promised you all of me...
That the secret places had your name
With keys engraved.
That no other friend or lover
Could replace
or take that space

You laid footprints...
Pitta patter life gathers
Pink bows... Who knows...?
Yeah what would it look like?
If I could love you complete.
In another lifetime...
Maybe... Badu said.
Instead...
What would it look like?
If I simply spoke... I love you.
Guess we'll never know.
So
This note will be my private message
Asking
What
Would
It
Look
Like....

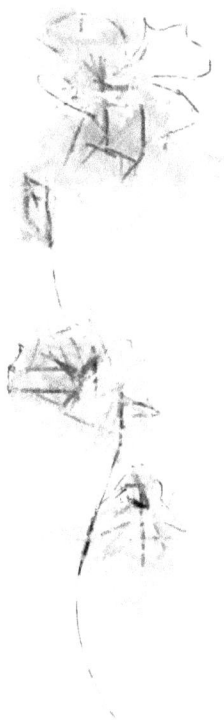

Stars An Observation

It's like in a past life they were stars
Playing in orbital dreams and enchanting each other with
discoveries shared
only and understood by them.
Evaporated time and shifts
Millions of ions away from their celestial playground
He broken by the past
She brimming with hopeful possibilities
They meet
And something unknown to the eye
Collides and spirit
Recognizes
This is that star
to mine.
Melting into each other
With lack of knowledge but ease
The intimacy of their bond
Fueled with charm and understanding
Neither knowing that the pattern was
Designed and set before they met.
Like best friends yet
More.
Like a love but closed doors.
Something so innocent
So pure.
The need to explore
But surrender to
The tender moment
of what is...
Never knowing the why's
Or how's ...
But living in the now...
Taking each breath as it comes
Stars reconnected now under the sun
Embracing in that space unseen
While he and she engage
Igniting orbital dreams...
They may never know
but spirits always know.

Lazy Day Chronicle Blues

Got me open
My body jones'ng
On fire times ten
Screaming please me
Tease me
Honey pot pleading
Feed me
Need me
On top of you
Pinch me
Taste me
Take me
Deep thrusts
Erection
Tip
must
Be touched
Make love
And fuck
Addicted it's true
What can I do?
When all I want is you.
Lazy day chronicle blues.

A Song A Thought

A song
A thought
pull out a hidden photo
Your face I stare
I crave the taste of your pain
Bury it in a place in me
Heal the broken that haunts you
My hands reach
To teach myself the memory
Of your touch
So much
I can't breathe
Longing to release
Hold you in the space where
Your soul unfolds into mine
The pain and pleasure
Together feels like a dream
So far from reality
Let me stay sleep
Where we can be
In synchronicity
Heart beats
See me where I am
hidden
See you where scars plague
Make love begs, our bodies
And mind free.
Look at me and see what I see
In you
Beauty too
Blinding my rationale
My senses are heightened
You, under my skin… trying to live in
My secret caverns of nectar
Sweet love wants to pour over
Moreover you.
And stop.
Can't keep dripping mist that
Can only be caught in a thought

Conjured between stolen moments
In time
Rivers flowing but never knowing
And that constant is much
More than I can
bare
Naked I stand defenseless
asking and resisting nothing
But yearning for more
So, I implore pen to page
To counter this stage…
And give way for/to escaping
The ache.
Tears.
Fall
Free
above
and
below.

Sleepless Nights

Late hours when it's quiet
I sometimes wonder if you can feel me thinking of you.
I rationalize with my thoughts debating with my heart to say nothing
Wrestling match with sleep, exhausted from fighting memories hovering over me.
night filled with bursting stars
Wanderer you are
sweetness of essence like smoke
filling my lungs, air
melodic cries from me escape
inside waters ache
a pleasure nondescript...
feeling?
Imprint like honey
bathing on every part of me.
flee and set me free
so, another can give me release.
My treasure is a hidden pleasure
addictive
us both
but I want most to toast a red glass with you
under skies deep blue/black
explore the unspoken for hours in our eyes and let the ecstasy rise.
Hieroglyphics is the language I speak
so arduous in the quest of what I seek
In this enormous land...needle in a haystack
for what moves me.
proves to me the right to experience what's sacred.
And yet you have taken...
or better yet I willfully have given....
you full license to possess the best
parts of my whole...
got a slice of my soul wrapped up in your palm
I want days on pause.... just so I could know the heart of you
show you what's true.
kiss and bite my delight
touch minds, play like bright flowers intertwined

40

in fields of unknown lands.
It seems so sweet to be ....
held in the mastery
of love making that has taken
physical conversation to my language
and....
and
I'll be alright...
just gotta get you out of my mind...

41

Medicinal Love

Through my scars I track bars
Send lessons and blessings to the stars.
No need to run from the sun, son
My charm isn't encapsulated to harm
But brings forth new...show the greater of you
My eyes
see how I see you
Light
And this passive aggressive running from demons
On this rat wheel masquerading is misleading
And bleeding you dry…
All your lies
to hide
And I see you.
No judgment and yet excepting nothing less than
Truth…
While looking at the man in the mirror
Talking about your fear of....
yet you are wearing that suit with
Tailored precision...
You can't heal what you don't reveal...
Cause even in your love
it's got your ego first
And my thirst is to know
if this was all a show...
And
Am I the first of many?
Cause from your own mouth you got plenty
Of reasons to uproot
With exception of your beautiful two.
And I love you...Enough to be your friend through
But something in the way you move... waxing poetic
Yet your actions create infractions on everyone you claim
Has fashions in your heart.
Broken king you didn't really see me...
Cause I grow roses out of concrete.
Yeah you had a gem beyond my sexual appetite.
I am bonafide of the body soul and mind
Cause that's what I do.

42

Would never let you settle to
The lowest part of you.
Your talk is surface because your soul got wounds
On top of wounds wearing masks
To pretend that influence isn't there.
And listen, I care. More than I should.
But I am no victim to you...
Rather a real friend to you...
Yeah you broke me and
Choked me with your attempt
To flip prints and make
me a problem in your high
But
I am the light come into your life
to show you
what you're hiding beneath
And endless possibilities.
But first you gotta be willing
To really see.
Pass my design that can induce lust
But focus on the trust
Cause another would have you on bust

Facts...
Track the trajectory

My mastery was not a manipulation
But a provocation of spiritual
Connect and reflect
Urging you to go to your deeper self
Move from empty to free
And I was unlocking that ability
Cause my intent when locked in
Searched for your higher
Even was a fighter trying to protect
The boundaries for you.
Grow in a space we can't even see
I am designed to elevate and illuminate
Attracted to light even in its dark.
But your still blind
With opened eyes

43

Getting lost in what's real
and what's a lie.
So, caught up in the perceptions
You're acting on deceptions
Breaking everything supportive in your path
Feeding on excessive levels of escapes
that rape and numb your mind

In time
it all catches up...

Then you're left asking what…?

Cause I was not a test to trap
But to reveal
Your real
Can you…?
Will you…?
Respect him enough? to accept him enough?
To heal him.

And I still love him.

Cause when I said I fell in love
That included your wounds.
From the jump I always saw
You.
Do you?
See?
Truth?

Loss is Loss
(pain, anger, sadness confusion, questions)
grief

45

For My Brother

What is light... By Websters dictionary it is the natural agent that stimulates sight and makes things visible.

Yes, light changes the atmosphere by illumination. Today we celebrate our ray of light, son, brother, nephew, cousin, family and friend.

I celebrate his victory. His win in the game of life and his light. I didn't always understand my brother's unique magnificence but as a late teen I began to see the beauty and I fully understood as an adult. I remember talking to him about a dog Reginald, we had when we were kids, at one of our holiday gatherings. Now as I recall Reginald was one of the meanest little dogs you would ever meet, he was notorious for barking and biting, but my brother spoke about Reginald with love and candor, while I went on a verbal assassination. He had the ability to find the good. This was part of his light. He didn't have it easy, and this life as challenging as it is to us, he faced challenges we could never and would never conceptualize... Yet, he walked victorious. He lived with love in his heart embracing people, extending smiles, and a devoted hugger. He loved teddy bears, the color blue, sunglasses, tea, CDs, clothes, he liked looking good, movies, DVDs, R&B music and money in his wallet. He loved his family and especially his mommy and his pretty aunties. Make no mistake my big brother loved beauty and no challenge would stop him from shooting his shot. He was not afraid to be transparent and honest, no matter the outcome, he led with love. "she's a nice girl, she is really pretty, her heart is beautiful." It was the childlike innocence and playfulness that not only drew people to him but gave him the boldness to be exactly himself, unashamed. Did he get disappointed and things not go his way? of course, but it never stopped him. He got up and danced to his Michael Jackson, Billie Jean and sang James brown wearing his sunglasses with passion because he loved it. Bottom line. It didn't matter the approval of others or if he even had the right words... most times he didn't which added to his charm. My goodness how my brother loved music. He could name every song and singer without batting an eye. "Bet you don't know who this is?'" that was his constant question when we had the music on. He and his two steps shake it moves. "ah ohh get it" mommy would say and he would bashfully laugh and say "come on pop" to daddy sitting in his favorite chair. These memories are so vivid because it was when I quietly marveled at his freedom to be. My brother wasn't shy about much of anything particularly when it came to his birthday… be clear we were all going to get a call at least a week before to remind us that it was coming up and he was expecting something special in the mail. I chuckled at this because secretly I think we all feel that, but he was bold enough to speak it. My brother loved Christmas and Jesus. He would tell me about church or ask if I went to church and want us to pray for him and others from time to time. He had that childlike faith.

"At that time the disciples came to Jesus, saying, "Who is the greatest in the kingdom of heaven?" And calling to him a child, he put him in the midst of them and said, "Truly, I say to you, unless you turn and become like children, you will never enter the kingdom of heaven. Whoever humbles himself like this child is the greatest in the kingdom of heaven. "Matthew 18:1-13 ESV

My brother lived this his entire life. The purity of him, the fearlessness of him came from his uniqueness. Just as young David in the Bible the most unlikely of all Jesse's sons, he killed Goliath because of his childlike faith.
My brother continuously slewed what we call Goliaths in this world. Fear, doubt, insecurity, judgment, approval seeking, agism, classism, etc. We are blinded, bound and succumb to the dark of this world but who my brother was/is was unfazed in the typical sense. We all have a purpose in this world, a divine assignment that God ordains of us. Sometimes we are aware of that purpose and sometimes our lives define that purpose. My brother's life was his purpose and your blessing if you're willing to open your eyes and see the message. His life proved limitations are a mindset. His life proved that you can, enjoy life and its many beautiful simplicities if you're willing. His life proved that you don't have to have it all to have it all. His life proved that joy is up to you, His life proved that love transcends, His life proved that you could try fall and get back up, His life proved that light will always penetrate the dark places. God blessed us to know my brother, to love him,

to witness his surpassing this world's rules and living a full thriving life outside the norm and yet exceptionally beautiful in its simplicity and honesty. Take a page from all he gave to us by living, and LIVE. Don't ignore it. But let it ignite you. Yes, my heart is so broken, and this is a pain I can't explain. But what I know, is, my brother is living golden without any constraints that this flawed world offers. He is with the Almighty. That is a priceless peace, that my flesh will need time to catch up to. He is bound by nothing. Let him be a sparkling wind beneath your wings. Let him be the beam of light on your cloudy day. Let my brother be your inspiration to live fully as he is mine.

His light doesn't dim but rather burns brighter by each one of you who carry everything he has shared and taught in his own special way.

I love you my sweet big brother. Your little big sister. Be free. Autism never stopped you and nothing should stop us.

I Never Stopped

Five thousand times in one day
Thirty-five thousand times in one week
That's how many times I try to release you
from me
It's like I can't breathe
Cause I'm holding my breath
Hugging my chest
Waiting and contemplating
Meditating on the past
And hoping this distance won't last.

But it seems like it's only me
Who's not free
So, I guess I need
To render surgery
Remove heart and mind from
Body.

It's like pulling life
from me
still born
Hearing the song before its played
And suddenly erased
As a figment of lines
Traced in a coloring book
In an unseen time and sky.

Did I dream it?
Did you mean it?

Cause in every tear I feel
the REAL
of hearts beating
Souls and pulses meeting in the spirit
and in the flesh.
I'm undressed with you...

All over me
And I

don't wanna flee
I never gave up on you and me
But wanted you to be released
from making a decision
That had created tortured fission's
In your mission to be so different
from him.

Wanted to give in
Everyday
Just to say
I love you
and I do
I need you
but I don't
so, I wont
but I want you
and I can't
wishing God had
other plans
and we could go back to holding hands
like innocent love on white sands
ending and beginning a new start
and nothing keeping us apart.
Forever in my heart
You are.

like you **really** are.
I'll be here **until** I'm **not.**

Time Is Bullshit

Time is real and its bullshit
I could pretend to save face
Act like there is no trace
Of your scent in my space
But why?
I tell no lies it doesn't change
My mind.
Out here on these streets
Brother's throwing "hey miss lady"
And I'm looking to annihilate
Like a beast
seeing prey
Praying that I don't lose my way
Cause I'm frustrated one day
On my calm
another
Sound the alarm...
My charm
Pulling them in.
But it ain't him...
And it's a game
I play
They can never win.

Be laying in these sheets
Hearing beats tempted to click and send
Legs waiting wide open and dripping
Debating with my want and tripping
Off my truth...
Fuck you and I fucks with you
Simultaneously on a speed and frequency
That lingers between push and pull
But I still want you
And I can't

Burn my incense to make some sense.
Chakras spinning through this
Rising smoke
Hoping that the inhale will transcend

51

Me to peace
Surrender my leash
back to the position
Of before you entered
And I lost my center.

It was like…like summer in winter.
And all of me is splintered into
A million particles of bliss lost
In a kiss that stays in a replay
Levitating on a puff puff pass
To myself.
This be a three dimensional high
That I've tried to hide and tie to
The ocean floor
Close the doors
Yet when it hits, I look up
and
Drift above...
to that place where time stands still
Locked in your smile
Locked in your eyes
Locked in your body
Locked in my mind
I don't wanna let you go.
Time's real
and
it's bullshit.

Rebel Fleur

The Gift

It's strange the flow of life
I never expected to
Find right
In wrong
But that's the song
Playing on my radio
It was like Christmas in spring
And I the child
Whose eyes opened wide
When I turned and saw your eyes
looking at mine.
Your smile.
That look that says a million things without speaking
But I can hear.
You were the gift.
The someone I missed
And wanted most
To see
My heart skipped beats
And I almost couldn't breathe
Cause there you were, right in front of me
Again
Could I freeze the frame?
Remove all the others
And be with you alone no shame
And claim the night as our own
I didn't know I would feel the same
And nothing had changed
For me
The revelation hit like a soft wind
I really am in love with him
Even mentioned by a friend...
And I didn't want the night to end.
But it did.

And I wanted to hold you a little tighter
Kiss you a little longer
Laugh with you a little harder
Talk a little deeper

Rebel Fleur

Make love to you slowly
Breathe- you- in- with- all- my- senses
Rest your cares on my heart
Tell you all the things unsaid
And unseen

And how much you really mean
Because when the door closed
And the silence hit
I realized I may never hear from
or see you again.

I love you
The Gift

Don't - A Waring Respectfully

Fall back before you try to attack
You don't know me or who I be.
And what you see is only what you perceive.
Cause when we break it down to basics
I....
Was the one aiming.
To keep things at bay.
And compassion is one with my soul but
Don't think I won't go
To the other side of the street.
Coming for me in your fear with displaced rage
Is a mistake you shouldn't make.
Cause I didn't send for you but rather fended for you
Indirectly...
This wasn't my pursuit and I knew I had to fight the tide
But it was his eyes
that didn't wanna let go
And eventually I gave in and let things flow
Cause love wanted to grow.
And even in the connection and intense affections
I never pulled that man into my direction.
But he walked
and moved willingly
beside me
Showing me, loving me, talking about babies and how
beautiful that would be.
Yeah.... don't come for me.
Never asked him for anything but my heart wanted everything.
and I was simmering in tears that I wouldn't show him
because I wanted him to grow in his own truth.
That means figuring out what he wants and needs to do.
Without me.
So we parted both of us broken hearted.
Letting go of what I wanted for
the greater good of HIS WHOLE.
Him with a HOLE so big and wounds so deep
Conflicted in his convictions to do what is right
Despite,
Talking about the emptiness in his heart there

and fullness of joy because I cared
feeling so complete in (our) we
Yeah... don't come for me.
Cause this is what I won't say
Trying to spare you the space
Of hearing what you don't really want to know
cause even when you were gonna go
His actions spoke.
Showing up to celebrate my life and
hell yeah I was surprised.
But I saw it in his eyes.
For a night, a peace, a freedom to be where he wanted to be
That's what he said to me
When questioned.
And even still I didn't mention…to put his attention to coming
my way.
I'm not leading this man astray.
Not trying to break up a happy home.
Didn't set up a seduction
That's not my induction for anything designed for me.
I let him move free and yeah, I'm a grown lady.
Since you wanna through indirect shade about my age
But it's my grade…
that knows a man does what he wants.
There is no coercion or diversion on my part
But a true heart that fell in love with a man
Who pursued my hand.
And even in resistance his persistence wore me down
Yeah, my crown is slightly crooked I'll admit
But I'm not owning shit
that ain't mine.
I wasn't competing but dealing with the meeting of the minds
that in time grew into more.
But the door I do not hold. It is his.
You are with him.
So, let go of this need to pull me into your mix
And get on your fix, to what you say you want
Cause trying to stunt on me and my reality
You should not do.
Do not come for me unless I send for you!
Yeah. All peace

What Is It?

What is it about him?
And yet again
I wander
With my heart in flux
Thinking I saw you on the street
I get stuck
Staring
Heart
rapid beats
Clenched fears and excitement
It's not him.
I'm shamed from a pain
I can't predict
When it hits
hard
I saw child in arms
And my alarm
Is why is this a trigger?
Go figure
womb, craving his seed?
Maybe
Insanity
Probably.
and it's all on me
To erase and release.
Purge the urge
Of communicating and demonstrating
Anything in my heart
Can't start on that road again
must be cold with him
he is not just my friend.
Though I'd like to believe.
I must let the slow process
of time demise or
give way for another to erase him
from my mind.

hold on me...

Roll The Dice

Sit at the table
Roll the dice
Did I play a game of lies?
And pay the price?
Inside my body and mind
I gave you the rights…
And I will always shine...
That is my divine
Yet the catch hits
Was this all on some fuck boy shit?
Legit was my bid
that made me give
What should have been reserved
To he that serves only me
Questions run so deep. Paralyzing me
In between understanding
Who you really be...?
Cause the one you find grace
The other I put you in your place
Disgraced is the taste you
Left to linger
On my fingers
held you
Like priceless treasure
The measures of imbalance
Screwing up my countenance
Cause I smile with a thought
Then I get caught wondering
Was it real?
Cause I get high in my thighs
Then I get tight
The way you took flight
Left me stuck on stupid
Say fuck you to cupid.
Cause tricks are for kids...
And I'm replaying on replay
all that shit you said and did.
Was it real...?
Cause I remember the feel

Of your eyes locked on me like
Life
And your stories written on my skin
I let you all the way in
To my soul.
You wanted to sleep in that space
Said you felt safe
Held me like you never wanted to let go
Replenished in my waters
Deplete me then delete me?
Cause you can't...?
What...?
Talk like a grown up
Sober up to face what's hard
Honor the connection with words of affection yet still do with
you must
That's what's called trust.
Yet you run
Smacked the emotional shit out of me
And danced into the sun...
Table for one...
I rolled the dice
And now I'm left to wonder did I ride with
A lie.

Rebel Fleur

Loop

Her soul is stuck in a loop
Understanding and not
Back and forth a rhythm
Like drums pounding her chest
a short breath escapes
With an ache that she doesn't know how to fix
Seeing the fall before the fall
doesn't remedy pain
She wants to fall into oblivion
the space before
where her heart felt nothing
when all were of no effect
her spirit untapped
Numb was freedom, no memories
Of her soul connecting
Songs bringing back a smile
her lips quick fade
a haze
Cloud covers it with grey
Take away
this hole that she can't explain
Chained to a part of her brain
That wants to replay...
Strength but tired
The loss. the costs
She needed no one and stood tall
But then the fall
Ripped down walls...
Revealing what she had been fleeing
Meeting of something that matters
She rather not.
Battle more than she could bare
On her ass emotionally
And her heart says she should have stayed free
Of jumping down the rabbit hole of
Dreams. Now what.
Fuck. She's stuck in this loop
Trying to figure out how to
Get loose.

Rebel Fleur

Thinking Of Eli

In the corner cavern of night when all is silent
The dance happens
New.
Nice to meet you... again, I dream.
Passing moons have left a distant hole yet inside
You have remained, unceasing.
To love still,
love... different yet the same...
love feels.
You are.
I am.
Love.
Scarlet letter branded on my chest
I feel.
Shackled to shame... my perception claims,
A yard stick kept between any moment that positions us near,
Unclear.
A 300-pound weight that allows no forward motion.
3650 plus days of soundless ambivalence
friends (?) today?
No expectations just be in the existing.
Have tea, see thee, see me…
In the evergreen blooming beauty of now.
But no sound…listless lifeless hummmmmmmmmm
of not comprehending what is the fault.
Disease?
Sickness?
Youthfulness?
Love?
Ruminating wonders.
But in the dark when the spirit runs free through the ether
of light,
And id, ego and super ego are on pause…
We laugh,
Smile,
Learn different.
3650 plus days the dream is all that feels real anymore.
Can't hold the intangible, elusive, so forge on.
Stand still…can't.

Rebel Fleur

But hope of a day that knocks and (h)open(ing) your eyes will be in the present.
Smacked ego in the name of truth I have nothing to lose.
That's how awareness changes when death ensues you.
No longer balancing the beam of tip toeing to sustain a crumb left from
A table rotted moons ago.
It looks back at me and says "don't pick me up"
"Sit at the table where you belong and expect a full meal because that's what you deserve."
But for 3650 plus days I picked, nibble, dusted off that crumb, the imagination greatly willing it to be a meal.
It's not.
Won't be made prisoner of what I can't undo.
The past bitches at me then I cradle her with care and politely say shut the fuck up.
Had to be and go through the pain to advance, grow on my own
Never intended to leave scars.
Let me pour some of my healing libation on what still hurts, I don't...
Growth brought today.
We could be gentle in our auras and touch by communicating honesty.
Simplicity
Complicate nothing... its easy
Hello I'm....
Nice to meet you.... I'm ...
And yet,
it is way surpassed those 3650 plus days I waited
15 years and the knowingness that life teaches the heart to adapt
Shift
Recognize the unfathomable possibility as just such
and live...
Then you did...show up
but
him...

Saying Goodbye Close The Door

Process the emotions. Say what's in your heart.
Whatever it is unrestricted.
Get it out of your system.
Face it.
Cry.
Be Angry.
Be Sad.
Be Frustrated.
Be Sentimental.
Be Sexual.
Be Kind.
Be Cruel.
Be Honest.
Be Raw.
Be Unashamed.
Be Shamed.
Be Free.
Be Open.
Be Closed
Be Whatever YOU NEED to be,
Pen it on the PAGES to HEAL and GET IT OUT.
THEN...
CLOSE THE DOOR.

The Coping Narrative?

Love letter to herself.
A heart that pierces like indigo flames
and radiance through the sky.
Often obliged to sit on a shelf.
Distant in conventions
To protect the fragility within
But with him she gave freely
Because she believed.
There is no casualty in her honesty.
Even if he was a fraud of deceit.
She will not be imprisoned to shame.
If it was his game
then brilliantly played.
Because she gave with no restraints
But rather poured and adored
The impostor.
Her heart gives no denial to her truth
But speaks it like harps on a
Silent day with an ocean breeze
Serene and clean
Majestic and infectious
New morning dew
With him she dreamt of everything
And never had a clue
That he was an artifice of truth.
There are days she wants to vanish from the inside out
Because if asked assuredly, she had no doubt
That love existed between them.
It was a balance of love and lust
And the depth of their touch
And laughing so much
...
She watched their feelings grow
Or perhaps just a show
On his part.
But he had her heart
And like gleaning sands in her hand
She never held on tight
but allowed for him to slip

Rebel Fleur

if he did not wish
To carry on the dance
Yet every chance...
He pulled her into a deeper level
Of his affections
She drinking his deceptions
As a gospel written just for her skin
She wanted to mend him, her lover and friend
She wanted to sing lullabies over his silent cries
And tell him he could see truth in her eyes.
That her love ran deep
The abyss in blue couldn't conceive.
But may she not find fault in her hearts
Blindness
And not judge her kindness as a personal indictment
But merely a reflection of the vastness of beauty within her
soul
when she believes.

The capacity to hold space for another
She wants safe
In her love.
She is capable of what he is not.
What is real...
He got
because that is who she is.
No need to apologize
That her heart fell in love with
A beautiful lie.

But she reflects gratitude from the blessing
Of a continued resurrection
To believe.

His part is up.
Now end scene.

Rebel Fleur

Nothing Fancy Facts

It could all be so simple
Just dismiss you
As inconsequential.
As a mistake, bad day.
Like you never existed
Someone I resisted.
A regret that I neglected
To admit
but once reflected
I can't
Truth is you took
Captivity over me
My heart is missing beats
Reminiscing on you and me
How do I not get lost?
So caught in my mind
When I don't even try
Having my…
Body
Shiver
A laugh escapes my lips
And tears run from my eyes
each time
I give focus to you
We smiled together like sunshine
Balanced intoxication
Beautiful expressions
Breathing each other in
Verbal intellect sparring jarring senses
Pass 10
Yeah, I'm jacked up
Spiritually I blame me
Should have kept the walls high
But every time I tried
You found another way in
To win
My heart
My body
My mind

You pursued relentless
till I surrendered
And engendered the tender
Of what I keep bury deep inside.
I know they say time heals
But I'm in my feels
hard
Over you.
Thinking on ways to have
even one more
Day around the sun
Wrapped up in you
Wanting to love on you
While planting dreams
damn the high you got me…
And as a queen I know what
I believe,
The best for me and nothing less
Yet
You haunt my thoughts
And my hurt is still raw
like an addiction withdrawal
beautiful ones pursue
From every corner
And all I'm bored of
While wondering if
You think of me when you're with her
As Sade says is it a crime
her kisses are certainly
Not like mine
Body in sync
We drink each other sublime.
I feel like I'm missing time
With someone so right for me
When it was
And my heart bleeds
Trying to surrender my confused need
And plead to myself
Remember the pain and
what truth I know
And just…let go.

Rebel Fleur

Confession

Maybe it's nothing
But it feels like something
How much do you know?
Of what I can't show.

Naked mind
Exposed
I want to be close
It's the
in between my breaths
When I can't catch
The image of you
without
Falling into the deep
Stuck in the heat
Longing for repeats
And you can't see.

Or can you?
maybe when you sleep
you meet me in dreams
that place
Where our reality can be
At least for me.

Cause for now I'm yours
Even with closed doors
You breeze through
Nothing I can do
But let you.

I'm tired of fighting and hiding
At least with myself

So, I stand still in the power
Of
Our connection
And let it wash over
Me like second skin

Rebel Fleur

Burning yearning
Delirium and ecstasy
Until my body peaks
Delicately...
Tears from each part of me
Cause how can it be
You have this much effect?
And there's no direct in
Which I can manifest
What my heart says it
Wants most.
Craving to have you close.

That face I can't replace
Sweeps a smile on
Me I can't erase.
And I hate
The power you take
I so willingly want to give.
My choice
Your voice
My love
Your heart
My body
Your key to my parts
Your mind
I can linger in with no matter of time
Your hurts
My womb where life blooms
I'm fixated
Tried to escape it
And I can't debate it.
I face it
I miss you
and I can't take it.

Black Lavender Hued Butterfly

Beautiful lavender hued black butterfly
On lookers get mesmerized
He got high off her
She
be
Anomaly of light
Yet he never took time
To see her fight
Pushing through the dirt and despair
Crawling on empty
Darkness in the air.
She never learned to really lean
Shoulders laid on with others and their dreams.
Healing vibrations exude from her wings
Fostering protection to the broken
Unknown
He's sown himself attached to her
Gathering strength from her love
So perfectly fit to restore
Brokenness in his brokenness
Enraptured by her kiss... His bliss
Milk and honey flavored peace
He feasts
on what he thought could never be
Sanctuary of dreams breathing life
Inhaling black lavender hued butterfly
She inhales with him...
Could this sage begin a new phase?
Giving and receiving
Of breathing
together.
He says he can stay here forever.
Cause he's feeling renewed by
What she can do to the wounds
Hiding in him deep.
He started to feel free...
And she
Like meadows plush in purple and greens
They jumped in with both hands and feet.

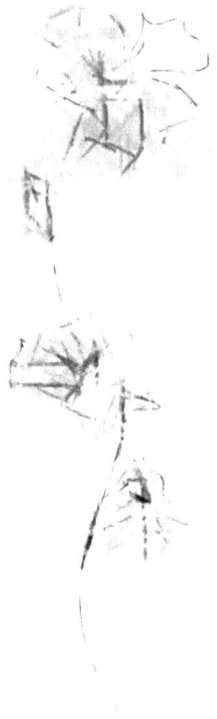

Rebel Fleur

Delightful, joy
Pure innocence in heart...
She made more space for him
to rest and lay
Renew then play.
Never knowing that her hue was
Going to be erased
Once he was filled and ready to run
His race.
Black lavender hued butterfly
Faded vibrancy
Love and confusion resting in her soul
Flutters with weak wings
Understanding why the cage bird sings…
Let her beauty only be seen
Never try to get next to she.
Protection in miss-direction...
No room for affection that takes to build
And leaves to die.
She will once again fly high
And higher still
Until
Touch is impossible.
Black lavender hued butterfly.

Rebel Fleur

Renewal and Revelations are essential tools of growth.

Unicorn

When I write sometimes it feels like my wings grow back.
From a premature clipping that lowered my frequency.
I write to heal, to understand, to grow, to build back up.
To have peace take residency in my soul, again.
So, I take a moment today from reading other pages to pen my
own.

She that is magnetized by things it finds rare
Contemplating she stared and let internal antennas guide
Holy spirit eyes.
Discernment beckons be wise.
And even with vetting upon vetting
One cannot predict
A touch, a word that penetrates beyond comprehension.
It isn't simple addition.
But fragments and fractions.
Hidden factions that the heart justifies…
Small compromise because there is no lie
In that ride…that has no explanation…
She visualized marvelous destinations
Give way to moments
Words paint pictures and speak life to the body and mind
Relaxed – comfort – teach – be taught
Try and be patient… the heart feels
It looks real
And nothing resonates falsely, but safe.
Unicorns are fantasy
but she is…
actually
heart pumping blood…
richly submerged in a sensual decadence but pure...
only the selected steps through
doors of layered protection
warding off affections of scorpions…neglecting
what's within.
Open…
Protecting…
Unguarded...
Wanting but limited…she stayed…in the distance…

…
uncertain of her…. experience in pieces…
no guarantees… need history…
make her a memory.
She became…
BLUNT force jolts, unexpected-she unprotected
(insert range of emotions here)
Silence: silence:
By a cherry blossom stream, she watched the red in her eyes stare back at her.
Recognition no matter infliction her heart spoke no lie.
She would not hide to save face, but retraced each tear with a moment of pleasure, prayer, love and laughter.
The beauty of the unicorn is it remains before and after.

Still A Woman

The lady adorned in suave, swagger, sexuality, sunflower
smiles, God's light and generous laughter.
She is anomaly and dichotomy. Strong, Warrior, Fighter,
Resilient, Brave and Bold.

But what if I told you that she is a warrior and resilient because
she has to be. Because to be anything else would destroy her.
That sometimes she wants to put down the assault weapons and
not fight.

What if I told you that she needs a chance to let fragility, her
fragility be revealed and held tight in an embrace of
understanding.

Survival of the fittest is a tiring race to run because people
begin to think she's invincible and
doesn't need like them,
she gives but still needs....
a place to be wounded and rest pieces of her firefly wings
where the soft side can breathe and be replenished.

Can you see her?
The secret place that wants to be loved just like everyone else.

Let not the fire of passion fool you, or the iron of a hardened
soul protected confuse you.

She is strong but indeed a woman.

Epilogue - God's Love

After the storm, God always finds a way of reminding us that
HE still loves us and is always in control. Pain is inevitable in
this life but trusting God and in HIS promises is the assurance
that the best for us is always HIS glory. When I have been hit
with tremendous pain, I have always found a gift and blessing
on the other side of it. But surrender is the only way I can get
to that side, of HIS divine grace. Surrender enables me to see
from a perspective that my humanity is blinded to. Where there
are no answers faith prevails. This has been a season of
nothing but faith while enduring enormous storms yet may I
add STILL STANDING...by HIS GRACE.

A new burst, star finds its way
Holding hands with the night
Glow
Spring dew
Love new
The beginnings
Day break
Beach ocean mist
First kiss bliss
It can be
Hope sprinkles from heavens eyes
Naked skin blushes at sunsets smile
Dance alone but not lonely
Pink sands paint pictures
Seasons change, endless possibilities
Of dreams reborn
Eyes like amber sing
A timeless tune
Beauty from ashes
Age created wisdom
Hold to nothing and everything
Loose fingers
Melodies whistle
Leaves applaud...
Nature serenade's
The splendor of resurrection.

Honorable Mentions

The First

What do you give the man who has the world at his disposal
for his birthday?
My answer?
Truth.
Of the splendor I see in you.
Celebration of the creation…every year waiting for the
moment I can confess,
Address how quietly I give thanks and pray to the heavens to
send you a blessing
Wrapped in my essence and perhaps when stillness meets you
Feeling a breeze, the small of your back you'll know simply
that a kiss was planted by me in prayer.
Every year I declare this ritual of mine.
For this day only…travel with me where time and space are of
no value.
I'll immerse you with words that speak from this being to
salute your divinity.
A King,
Indeed, but more I believe, in verity most vocabulary has
inadequacies
At least in my defining you.
For on this unknown planet.... just for today I'll greet thee
With an introduction to the woman who speaks freely
And moves boldly.
No ego just bare I stared into the eyes of your youthful aura
when last I saw and observed,
man, of quiet mystery
Not enigma…because I see.
Weak in the knees, we became, no shame.
The girl in me tickled flushed in pink.
I'll join with your laughter.
Tease like school children making songs no other can
comprehend.
Enchanted being you send energies of light that touch the souls
willing to receive.
Giver and sometimes depleted because the reservoir of light
seeks replenishment,
Too strong to commence to verbal admit so in this dwelling lay
your head quietly with me and be.

Everything is everything.
I need not be told...know you are safe in this element if just for today.
I'll celebrate the truth the true the bare bones you.
The wonderful complexity of man and young man, depth and frivolity.
Incense flowing from his fro, revolutionary mind of intellect, listening to Hendrix and Bach at sunset,
Guitar keys and djembe hands, libations of brown, travel the world unlocking discoveries, quoting Yeshua in Hebrew, playing in the sun with a hymn of psalm 23 humming from your lips.
I will kiss an ode of thankfulness to who you are...
Star beyond common limitations applied to the word.
I know your soul...lion and dove made love and there was it born.
You're both light and dark equally beautiful.
It is the paradoxes of all the in-between polar that is gloriously intriguing.
Be free...
Decadent passions that may incur the soul to hide...
I'll breathe them with you.
Tantric breaths ... Breathe in and out...
I celebrate you... Can you feel?
The meadows are fresh and new.
I'll let this affection exist in this atmosphere.
Unknown to man, time or boundaries it has surpassed, breathing on this unknown planet.
Stripped down...
To simplicity.... wanting you to be freely adored on your day of birth...
For the totality of yo"u"r uniqueness.
So, I expose and present
A chess board with two glasses of wine. A lowly saxophone.
I will dance for you, with you. Patchouli surrounds the senses
Venus illuminates...
I'll write you a symphony of movement in your name...
Each sway is a note of gratitude to every lesson and blessing you have brought, taught
Known and unknown.
Because I want you to know if only for today...

You are a Van Gogh of your very own.
There is no replica, carbon copy,
That God stamped his extra dose of something specifically His on your being.
Mesmerizing from at first introduction beyond superficial givens.
Sustaining like a potion that leaves you drunk and elevated with joy simultaneously.
Original and head strong to be you, moving to beats only you create, when you decide.
You are ….
And if only for today…close your eyes
Where a celebration awaits
To Give,
To Share
To Delight
To Listen
To Laugh
To Dance
With you and for you dripped in love. **The First.**

(Written 2012)

The Second

Beauty from the first left me reserved
And knowing what I deserved
Bar high, I was able to preserve
me.
Years elapsed
I loved, not fully.
Saw the end as it began.
My investments, no roots.
Something always amiss.
But content to be my best for me
Working and blooming my dreams
Romance not on my scene
By choice.
Not interested in wasting energy
On sheer novelty.
Artificial in these streets.
Then...
You.

Kindred effortless flow
Stopped in my path.
Moving with the rhythm of our vibe
Days upon days and then into nights
Something was growing
That I couldn't deny.
Imperfectly, beautiful.
Your stories of life
Holding my hands in prayer
The way you shared, transparent.
There was comfort and familiar.
Sapiosexual minds dancing equally
Intrigued by your aura:
Gentle, strong and the countless colors of in-between.
Paralleled mine:
Playing like children in stores or kitchen floors
Philosophizing like old souls
Laughing like lifetime friends
Loving like spirits that encountered before
Passion like two people specifically intended for each other.

Talking with truth like trust had always been.
Kissing like lips that had a road map of our desires.
Trial and error never required.
Unlocking pieces of me.
Unlocking pieces of you.
The fit.
I fell in love. You didn't believe.

We embarked and I experienced loves possibilities.
Your essence ignited the nurturer in me naturally
Yearning to give and dispense love into all of you.
My spirit became yours without my concession.
Crimson patterns of sonnets chase the winds
Honoring both broken shadows of a shooting star
come and gone
And the bravery of being touched.
By what seemed impossible…
Love
Carved out of the unintended but written.
Like blazing orange and tranquil purple on the horizon
Colliding with you, created a brilliant hue that
I thought forgotten.
I will not erase you or negate you
But rather be in awe of the space between
When you looked at me and I looked at you
And all knowingness was said.
And we surrendered
Tender.
The heart wants what it wants.
Your head rested on my lap
Your fingers traced the patterns on my nose.
Love had grown in those moments of unspoken… words
Like fingerprints etched
with an undeniable tailoring to me.
Uniquely distinct.
You exist within.
I fell. Deeply. **The Second.**

Hope

Listless lifeless ideas float for a home
Candled quiet moments search for existence
The air is heavy
We breathe out hope
Even while inhaling doubt
Mangled hearts and innocent wide eyes
Find a resting place.

Chance, the jester to such fragile forms
Madness and despair try to take dominion
As they are cohorts in the mind's army.
Silence take up the sword of promise.
Resist the torrent winds, stand planted.
Forest of dreams.
Invite whispers from the east heavens to soothe…
Saline devices that discourage.

Hidden in the lace lit breast
Raging with rapid pulse
Lives the time-stricken creature
Of our affections.

Bleeds, breathes not deadened
Still holding the power of probability.
It is a friend that reminds us
Life is still ours...
Saccharine still encourages lips to smile
New is constant in change
Beautiful can be again.
Our mandala has not stopped.
Open
We begin again.
Love we do, Love we will.
Life anew.

Rebel Fleur

I Am Not Alone - Thank You To The Poet

I was loved in a time before I existed in the flesh.
Seeing the spirit emanate glowing reams of light blinding
Waves off eternal emerald seas coasting tropical shores.
You bellowed expressions versed in enigmatic cryptograms
That tripped synthesis in the cosmos only I could understand.
Metaphysically I laid within the shores and sands where you
spoke.
Swallowing each ripple lodging my appetite on every syllable
Bottomless black hole clung our moments
Thirsting to be filled from envy
Voracious urgencies made love in the turbulent thrashings
Aquatic ripping rocks, lapping sea creatures chuckle with
delirium.
The copulation heightened from every phrase shared as my
pink earth gathered warmly for your walking foundations.
My wet serene calming the heat of your skin
Cooing birds hum with me the tune of thanksgiving
You languished in the light loving me more by verse.
Aloof was a foreign word as you poured out the honey of your
affections
Pure, gazing and exposing to each page.
At the altar of my seas revealing you
And the time passed…we laughed
And the time passed… we loved
And the time passed… peace pursued,
and deaths angels enveloped you
To the islands of endless time.
Life gave birth to me, a woman outstretched
Searching in a land of tombs of love and caskets of passion
Stumbling over cobwebs of acceptance and honesty I walked
And wrestled with discontent
Beating and bleeding myself from the gnawing within
Stumbling over, stumbling over, then
Stumbling over frayed rustic white pages haphazardly resting
at the bottom of a shelf.
Forgotten
Anguish led with tenderness to reach and receive
Memories of a past life
seemingly familiar reverberate off every

84

Black etched out letter to form words.
It was him... the lover... having left words documented.
Gasping lambency shown all over my carriage and warmth settled my soul.
Orchid like beauty filled my thoughts as every page turned.
Finding rest by the sea, freeing all my golden flesh under the amber skies uninhibited, unashamed.
Submerging whole self in the ocean frolicking over sands covered in the essence of what I knew was true.
Pausing I smiled at the half gleaming moon playing peekaboo with the setting sun
And praised.
Then with a small luminous tear from the corner of my eye...
I uttered thank you to the poet and the likes of you
for understanding hearts like mine.
And creating works that speaks to the fabric of my spirit.
You get me
And I thank you.

Rebel Fleur

Afterword

Quarantined yes, but my mind and spirit are free to express,
roam and soar above any space.
I will not give way to fear of what I cannot control.
But rather find peace in expressions rooted in love.
I choose. I chose.
And I graciously
thank you for sharing.

Rebel Fleur
Loss Love & Life
Quarantined Musings of a Thug Dove
Copyright © 2020
ISBN- 978-0578690056

Simple complex messy beautiful ugly honest raw painful flawed powerful

And every color of the rainbow

These pages and this book are my survival and method of coping
my heart in your hands

This is the transformation of pain into purpose

.

*I am **love** looking back at **you.***

www.ingramcontent.com/pod-product-compliance
Lightning Source LLC
Chambersburg PA
CBHW071420040426
42445CB00012BA/1223